Everything You Ever Wanted to Know About...

Everything You Ever Wanted to Know About....

Absolutely nothing, because we really don't care...

Everything You Ever Wanted to Know About...

Absolutely nothing, because we really don't care...

Everything You Ever Wanted to Know About...

Absolutely nothing, because we really don't care...

Everything You Ever Wanted to Know About...

Absolutely nothing, because we really don't care...

Everything You Ever Wanted to Know About...

Absolutely nothing, because we really don't care...

Everything You Ever Wanted to Know About...

Absolutely nothing, because we really don't care...

Everything You Ever Wanted to Know About...

Absolutely nothing, because we really don't care...

Everything You Ever Wanted to Know About...

Absolutely nothing, because we really don't care...

Everything You Ever Wanted to Know About...

Absolutely nothing, because we really don't care...

Everything You Ever Wanted to Know About...

Absolutely nothing, because we really don't care...

Everything You Ever Wanted to Know About...

Absolutely nothing, because we really don't care...

Everything You Ever Wanted to Know About...

Absolutely nothing, because we really don't care....

Everything You Ever Wanted to Know About....

Absolutely nothing, because we really don't care...

Everything You Ever Wanted to Know About...

Absolutely nothing, because we really don't care.....

Everything You Ever Wanted to Know About.....

Absolutely nothing, because we really don't care...

Everything You Ever Wanted to Know About...

Absolutely nothing, because we really don't care...

Everything You Ever Wanted to Know About...

Absolutely nothing, because we really don't care...

Everything You Ever Wanted to Know About...

Absolutely nothing, because we really don't care...

Everything You Ever Wanted to Know About...

Absolutely nothing, because we really don't care...

Everything You Ever Wanted to Know About...

Absolutely nothing, because we really don't care...

Everything You Ever Wanted to Know About...

Absolutely nothing, because we really don't care...

Everything You Ever Wanted to Know About...

Absolutely nothing, because we really don't care...

Everything You Ever Wanted to Know About...

Absolutely nothing, because we really don't care...

Everything You Ever Wanted to Know About...

Absolutely nothing, because we really don't care...

Everything You Ever Wanted to Know About...

Absolutely nothing, because we really don't care...

Everything You Ever Wanted to Know About...

Absolutely nothing, because we really don't care...

Everything You Ever Wanted to Know About...

Absolutely nothing, because we really don't care...

Everything You Ever Wanted to Know About...

Absolutely nothing, because we really don't care...

Everything You Ever Wanted to Know About...

Absolutely nothing, because we really don't care...

Everything You Ever Wanted to Know About...

Absolutely nothing, because we really don't care...

Everything You Ever Wanted to Know About...

Absolutely nothing, because we really don't care...

Everything You Ever Wanted to Know About...

Absolutely nothing, because we really don't care...

Everything You Ever Wanted to Know About...

Absolutely nothing, because we really don't care...

Everything You Ever Wanted to Know About...

Absolutely nothing, because we really don't care....

Everything You Ever Wanted to Know About....

Absolutely nothing, because we really don't care...

Everything You Ever Wanted to Know About...

Absolutely nothing, because we really don't care...

Everything You Ever Wanted to Know About...

Absolutely nothing, because we really don't care...

Everything You Ever Wanted to Know About...

Absolutely nothing, because we really don't care...

Everything You Ever Wanted to Know About...

Absolutely nothing, because we really don't care...

Everything You Ever Wanted to Know About....

Absolutely nothing, because we really don't care...

Everything You Ever Wanted to Know About....

Absolutely nothing, because we really don't care...

Everything You Ever Wanted to Know About...

Absolutely nothing, because we really don't care...

Everything You Ever Wanted to Know About...

Absolutely nothing, because we really don't care...

Everything You Ever Wanted to Know About...

Absolutely nothing, because we really don't care...

Everything You Ever Wanted to Know About...

Absolutely nothing, because we really don't care...

Everything You Ever Wanted to Know About...

Absolutely nothing, because we really don't care.....

Everything You Ever Wanted to Know About.....

Absolutely nothing, because we really don't care...

Everything You Ever Wanted to Know About...

Absolutely nothing, because we really don't care...

Everything You Ever Wanted to Know About...

Absolutely nothing, because we really don't care...

Everything You Ever Wanted to Know About...

Absolutely nothing, because we really don't care...

Everything You Ever Wanted to Know About...

Absolutely nothing, because we really don't care...

Everything You Ever Wanted to Know About...

Absolutely nothing, because we really don't care...

Everything You Ever Wanted to Know About...

Absolutely nothing, because we really don't care...

Everything You Ever Wanted to Know About...

Absolutely nothing, because we really don't care...

Everything You Ever Wanted to Know About...

Absolutely nothing, because we really don't care...

Everything You Ever Wanted to Know About...

Absolutely nothing, because we really don't care...

Everything You Ever Wanted to Know About...

Absolutely nothing, because we really don't care...

Everything You Ever Wanted to Know About...

Absolutely nothing, because we really don't care....

Everything You Ever Wanted to Know About.....

Absolutely nothing, because we really don't care...

Everything You Ever Wanted to Know About...

Absolutely nothing, because we really don't care...

Everything You Ever Wanted to Know About...

Absolutely nothing, because we really don't care....

Everything You Ever Wanted to Know About...

Absolutely nothing, because we really don't care...

Everything You Ever Wanted to Know About...

Absolutely nothing, because we really don't care...

Everything You Ever Wanted to Know About...

Absolutely nothing, because we really don't care...

Everything You Ever Wanted to Know About...

Absolutely nothing, because we really don't care...

Everything You Ever Wanted to Know About...

Absolutely nothing, because we really don't care....

Everything You Ever Wanted to Know About....

Absolutely nothing, because we really don't care...

Everything You Ever Wanted to Know About...

Absolutely nothing, because we really don't care...

Everything You Ever Wanted to Know About...

Absolutely nothing, because we really don't care...

Everything You Ever Wanted to Know About...

Absolutely nothing, because we really don't care...

Everything You Ever Wanted to Know About...

Absolutely nothing, because we really don't care...

Everything You Ever Wanted to Know About...

Absolutely nothing, because we really don't care...

Everything You Ever Wanted to Know About...

Absolutely nothing, because we really don't care...

Everything You Ever Wanted to Know About...

Absolutely nothing, because we really don't care...

Everything You Ever Wanted to Know About...

Absolutely nothing, because we really don't care......

Everything You Ever Wanted to Know About...

Absolutely nothing, because we really don't care...

Everything You Ever Wanted to Know About...

Absolutely nothing, because we really don't care...

Everything You Ever Wanted to Know About...

Absolutely nothing, because we really don't care....

Everything You Ever Wanted to Know About...

Absolutely nothing, because we really don't care...

Everything You Ever Wanted to Know About...

Absolutely nothing, because we really don't care...

Everything You Ever Wanted to Know About...

Absolutely nothing, because we really don't care...

Everything You Ever Wanted to Know About...

Absolutely nothing, because we really don't care...

Everything You Ever Wanted to Know About...

Absolutely nothing, because we really don't care...

Everything You Ever Wanted to Know About...

Absolutely nothing, because we really don't care...

Everything You Ever Wanted to Know About...

Absolutely nothing, because we really don't care...

Everything You Ever Wanted to Know About...

Absolutely nothing, because we really don't care...

Everything You Ever Wanted to Know About...

Absolutely nothing, because we really don't care...

Everything You Ever Wanted to Know About...

Absolutely nothing, because we really don't care...

Everything You Ever Wanted to Know About...

Absolutely nothing, because we really don't care...

Everything You Ever Wanted to Know About...

Absolutely nothing, because we really don't care....

Everything You Ever Wanted to Know About....

Absolutely nothing, because we really don't care...

Everything You Ever Wanted to Know About...

Absolutely nothing, because we really don't care...

Everything You Ever Wanted to Know About...

Absolutely nothing, because we really don't care...

Everything You Ever Wanted to Know About...

Absolutely nothing, because we really don't care...

Everything You Ever Wanted to Know About...

Absolutely nothing, because we really don't care...

Everything You Ever Wanted to Know About...

Absolutely nothing, because we really don't care...

Everything You Ever Wanted to Know About...

Absolutely nothing, because we really don't care...

Everything You Ever Wanted to Know About...

Absolutely nothing, because we really don't care...

Everything You Ever Wanted to Know About...

Absolutely nothing, because we really don't care...

Everything You Ever Wanted to Know About...

Absolutely nothing, because we really don't care...

Everything You Ever Wanted to Know About...

Absolutely nothing, because we really don't care...

Everything You Ever Wanted to Know About...

Absolutely nothing, because we really don't care...

Everything You Ever Wanted to Know About...

Absolutely nothing, because we really don't care...

Everything You Ever Wanted to Know About...

Absolutely nothing, because we really don't care...

Everything You Ever Wanted to Know About...

Absolutely nothing, because we really don't care...

Everything You Ever Wanted to Know About...

Absolutely nothing, because we really don't care...

Everything You Ever Wanted to Know About...

Absolutely nothing, because we really don't care...

Everything You Ever Wanted to Know About...

Absolutely nothing, because we really don't care...

Everything You Ever Wanted to Know About...

Absolutely nothing, because we really don't care...

Everything You Ever Wanted to Know About...

Absolutely nothing, because we really don't care...

Everything You Ever Wanted to Know About...

Absolutely nothing, because we really don't care...

Everything You Ever Wanted to Know About...

Absolutely nothing, because we really don't care...

Everything You Ever Wanted to Know About...

Absolutely nothing, because we really don't care...

Everything You Ever Wanted to Know About...

Absolutely nothing, because we really don't care...

Everything You Ever Wanted to Know About...

Absolutely nothing, because we really don't care...

Everything You Ever Wanted to Know About...

Absolutely nothing, because we really don't care...

Everything You Ever Wanted to Know About...

Absolutely nothing, because we really don't care...

Everything You Ever Wanted to Know About...

Absolutely nothing, because we really don't care...

Everything You Ever Wanted to Know About...

Absolutely nothing, because we really don't care...

Everything You Ever Wanted to Know About....

Absolutely nothing, because we really don't care...

Everything You Ever Wanted to Know About...

Absolutely nothing, because we really don't care…..

Everything You Ever Wanted to Know About...

Absolutely nothing, because we really don't care...

Everything You Ever Wanted to Know About...

Absolutely nothing, because we really don't care...

Everything You Ever Wanted to Know About...

Absolutely nothing, because we really don't care...

Everything You Ever Wanted to Know About...

Absolutely nothing, because we really don't care...

Everything You Ever Wanted to Know About...

Absolutely nothing, because we really don't care...

Everything You Ever Wanted to Know About...

Absolutely nothing, because we really don't care...

Everything You Ever Wanted to Know About...

Absolutely nothing, because we really don't care...

Everything You Ever Wanted to Know About...

Absolutely nothing, because we really don't care...

Absolutely nothing at all, because we really don't care...

Made in the USA
Monee, IL
26 June 2022

98669601R00075